First World War
and Army of Occupation
War Diary
France, Belgium and Germany

24 DIVISION
Divisional Troops
Royal Army Medical Corps
Divisional Field Ambulance Workshop Unit
31 August 1915 - 31 March 1916

WO95/2203/1

Published by

The Naval & Military Press Ltd

Unit 10 Ridgewood Industrial Park,

Uckfield, East Sussex,

TN22 5QE England

Tel: +44 (0) 1825 749494

www.naval-military-press.com

www.nmarchive.com

This diary has been reprinted in facsimile from the original. Any imperfections are inevitably reproduced and the quality may fall short of modern type and cartographic standards.

© Crown Copyright
Images reproduced by permission of The National Archives, London, England, 2015.

Contents

Document type	Place/Title	Date From	Date To
Heading	This item has been conserved as part of the WO95 Digitisation Project Please keep this sheet at the front of the box		
Heading	WO95/2203/1		
Heading	24th Fd. Amb. Work'p Unit Sep 1915-Mar 1916		
Heading	24th Division 24th. F.A Workshop Unit Sep 1915-Mar 1916		
War Diary	Roven	31/08/1915	03/09/1915
War Diary	Neufchatel	04/09/1915	04/09/1915
War Diary	Montieuil	05/09/1915	05/09/1915
War Diary	Beaurainville	06/09/1915	07/09/1915
War Diary	Neuville	08/09/1915	22/09/1915
War Diary	Radinghem	22/09/1915	22/09/1915
War Diary	Burzecor	23/09/1915	23/09/1915
War Diary	Berguette	24/09/1915	24/09/1915
War Diary	Bethune	25/09/1915	25/09/1915
War Diary	Benvry	26/09/1915	28/09/1915
War Diary	Annezin	29/09/1915	29/09/1915
War Diary	St Hilaire	30/09/1915	02/10/1915
Heading	24th Division 24th F.A.W.U. Vol 2 Oct 15		
War Diary	Steenvoorde	02/10/1915	03/10/1915
War Diary	Renninghelst	03/10/1915	01/11/1915
Heading	24th Div		
War Diary	Tilques	01/12/1915	31/12/1915
Heading	24th Division Nov 15		
War Diary	Renninghelst	01/11/1915	22/11/1915
War Diary	Steenvoorde	23/11/1915	23/11/1915
War Diary	Tilques	25/11/1915	30/11/1915
Heading	24th F.A. W.u.		
War Diary	Tilques	01/01/1916	07/01/1916
War Diary	Poperinghe	31/01/1916	31/01/1916
Heading	24th Div F.A.W.U.		
War Diary	No 17 Ca Charing Station	01/02/1916	29/02/1916
Heading	24 Div F A W U Vol 7		
War Diary	17 Cas Cleaning Stn	01/03/1916	23/03/1916
War Diary	Fletre	30/03/1916	30/03/1916
War Diary	Bailleul	31/03/1916	31/03/1916

This item has been conserved as part of the WO95 Digitisation Project

Please keep this sheet at the front of the box

W095/2203/1

24TH DIVISION
MEDICAL

24
~~74~~TH FD.AMB.WORK'P UNIT
SEP 1915- MAR 1916

24TH DIVISION
MEDICAL

12/7/31

24th Division

24th F.A. Brigade HQ Unit
Vol I

Sept. 15.
Mar '16

Sept 1915

Army Form C. 2118.

24th F.A.M.U

WAR DIARY
or
INTELLIGENCE SUMMARY.
(Erase heading not required.)

Instructions regarding War Diaries and Intelligence Summaries are contained in F. S. Regs., Part II. and the Staff Manual respectively. Title pages will be prepared in manuscript.

Place	Date 1915	Hour	Summary of Events and Information	Remarks and references to Appendices
Rouen	31/8	7.0am	Arrived and disembarked	
"	31.8	8.0.	Marched to Camp at Croix-de-la-Reine	
"	31.8	10.0.	Medical Inspection	ADg 2 D.
"	31.9	2.0pm	Inoculation	
"	1-9	9.0am	Kit Inspection	ADg
"	1-9	2.0pm	General Parade.	ADg
"	2-9	9.0am	Drawing petrol, stores, &c.	
"	2-9	2.0pm	Car and Engine inspection	
"	3-9	9.0am	General Parade.	ADg.
"	3-9	4.0pm	Left Rouen arrived at Neufchatel 7-0 pm	
Neufchatel	4.9	8.0am	Left Neufchatel arrived at Abbeville 1-0 pm halted for dinner and proceeded to Montreuil arriving at 4-0 pm	ADg

2353 Wt. W2544/1434 700,000 5/15 D.D.& L. A.D.S.S./Forms/C. 2118.

C. 2118. 2nd 7 A M U Army Form C. 2118

WAR DIARY
or
INTELLIGENCE SUMMARY.
(Erase heading not required.)

Instructions regarding War Diaries and Intelligence Summaries are contained in F. S. Regs., Part II. and the Staff Manual respectively. Title pages will be prepared in manuscript.

Place	Date 1915	Hour	Summary of Events and Information	Remarks and references to Appendices
Montreal	5-9	2.30pm	Left Montreal arrived at Beauxnville at 4.30pm	M.O.G.
Beauxnville	6-9	9.0am	General inspection of Cars and Engines.	M.O.G.
"	7-9	8.0am	Left Beauxnville arrived at Newville 9.30am	M.O.G.
Newville	8-9	9.0am	Ambulance and workshop staff on duty	M.O.G.
"	9-9	"	- do -	M.O.G.
"	10-9	"	- do -	M.O.G.
"	11-9	"	- do -	M.O.G.
"	12-9	"	- do -	M.O.G.
"	13-9	"	No 1. 2 & 3rd Ambulance sections transferred to 72nd, 73rd and 74th Corps Field Ambulance R.A.M.C.	M.O.G.
"	14-9		Workshop staff on duty	M.O.G.

2353 Wt. W2544/1454 700,000 5/15 D. D. & L. /A.D.S.S./Forms/C. 2118.

Army Form C. 2118

24th JWU

WAR DIARY
or
INTELLIGENCE SUMMARY.

(Erase heading not required.)

Instructions regarding War Diaries and Intelligence Summaries are contained in F. S. Regs., Part II. and the Staff Manual respectively. Title pages will be prepared in manuscript.

Place	Date 1915	Hour	Summary of Events and Information	Remarks and references to Appendices
Neuville	15.9	4.30am	General turn out at "Alarm" sounding.	ADg.
"	15.9	9.0am	Workshop staff on duty.	ADg
"	16th	2.15	- do -	ADg.
"	22nd	11.45am	Left Neuville arrived at Rabingham 2.30pm	ADg
Rabingham	22.9	9.30pm	Left Rabingham arrived Burzecor	ADg
Burzecor	23.9	1.15am	Left Burzecor arrived at Berguette 2.0am.	ADg
Berguette	24.9	6.0pm	Left Berguette arrived at Bethune 8.30pm	ADg.
Bethune	25.9	3.0pm	Left Bethune and halted on the Beuvry Road at 4.30pm	ADg
Beuvry Rd	26.9 & 27th		Workshop staff on duty	ADg
Beuvry Rd	28.9	4.30pm	Left Beuvry Rd arrived Annezin at 10.45 pm	ADg.
Annezin	29.9	4.30pm	Left Annezin arrived at St Hilaire 6.45pm.	ADg

Army Form C. 2118

24ᵃ F.A.W.C

WAR DIARY
or
INTELLIGENCE SUMMARY.
(Erase heading not required.)

Instructions regarding War Diaries and Intelligence Summaries are contained in F. S. Regs., Part II. and the Staff Manual respectively. Title pages will be prepared in manuscript.

Place	Date 1915	Hour	Summary of Events and Information	Remarks and references to Appendices
St Hilaire	30-9	5.1-10	St Hilaire Workshop Staff on duty.	MSg.
"	2-10	2.30pm	Left St Hilaire and arrived Steenwoorde 7.30 pm	MSg.

A.S. Gauntlett, Lt.
O.C. 24ᵗʰ F.A.W.C.

12/7608

24th Hussars

24th J.A.W.U.
Vol 2

Oct 15

Oct. 1915

Q.181.

Army Form C. 2118.

WAR DIARY
or
INTELLIGENCE SUMMARY.
(Erase heading not required.)

1 Sheet.

Instructions regarding War Diaries and Intelligence Summaries are contained in F. S. Regs., Part II. and the Staff Manual respectively. Title pages will be prepared in manuscript.

Place	Date	Hour	Summary of Events and Information	Remarks and references to Appendices
Steenwoorde	2-10-15		Workshop staff on duty.	MSg: "d" 20.
"	3-10-15	2/37pm	Left Steenwoorde and arrived Reninghelst 4.30pm	MSg: "d" 20.
Reninghelst 15 31-10			Workshop staff carrying out necessary repairs to Ambulance Motor Cycles. Lorries &c.	MSg: "d" 20.
— do —	1-11		— do — Remaining — do —	MSg: "d" 20.

H S Gamble. 2nd Lieut A.S.C. M.T.
O/c 17th Division I.A.M.W.

2353 Wt. W3544/1454 700,000 5/15 D. D. & L. A.D.S.S./Forms/C. 2118.

24th F.A.W.D.
vol. 4
Dec.

24th Div

Dec 1915

Army Form C. 2118.

WAR DIARY
or
INTELLIGENCE SUMMARY.

24th Div. F.A.W.U.

(Erase heading not required.)

Place	Date	Hour	Summary of Events and Information	Remarks and references to Appendices
Illsues	Dec 1st to Dec 31st Illsues.		Distilling Issues. Workshop staff carrying out repairs to Motor Ambulances, Motor Cycles etc. The matter during the past month has been fairly good and the location of the unit has not caused much inconvenience. Ambulances on the whole are running fairly well with the exception of broken travel wheels, and spring centre pins. The two former complaints are attributed to the overloading and as this has now been brought to the notice of those concerned I do not anticipate trouble in this direction in future. Regarding spring centre pins I would suggest that a great deal of trouble would be avoided if there were made of larger diameter and longer rods were fitted to the Ambulances. I have also experienced some considerable trouble in obtaining spare parts from M.T. Depot. & travel wheels, having to forward these, and it would greatly expedite matters if these could be despatched quicker. H.B. Granville 2nd Lieut A.S.C.	% 24th Div. F. Amb. W/Shop Unit

2 H. 2. a. o. o.
vol: 3

121/7656

only

24th H Braun

Nov 15

Nov. 1915

Army Form C. 2118

WAR DIARY
or
INTELLIGENCE SUMMARY.
(Erase heading not required.)

Instructions regarding War Diaries and Intelligence Summaries are contained in F. S. Regs., Part II. and the Staff Manual respectively. Title pages will be prepared in manuscript.

Place	Date 1915	Hour	Summary of Events and Information	Remarks and references to Appendices
Renninghelst	1-11-15		Workshop staff on duty repairing Ambulances &c.	
do	22/11	6.0 pm	Left Renninghelst & arrived Steenwoorde 9.0 pm. (Foggy weather).	
Steenwoorde	23/11	11.0 am	Left Steenwoorde & arrived Lederzeele 2.30 pm	
Lederzeele	24/11	3.0 pm	Left Lederzeele & arrived Ilgues 7.0 pm.	
Ilgues	25/11 to 30/11		Distillery Ilgues - Workshop staff on duty.	

H S Jarrell
2nd Lieut A.S.C.
% 1st Div. F. A. W. Unit.

24th F.A.W.U.
Vol. 5
Jan. 16.

Jan 1916

Army Form C. 2118.

WAR DIARY
or
INTELLIGENCE SUMMARY.
(Erase heading not required.)

24th Div. 7 Amb W/Shop Unit

Place	Date	Hour	Summary of Events and Information	Remarks and references to Appendices
Vlignes	1-1-16 to 7-1-16		2 Workshop staff repairing Ambulances to as necessary.	
Elzenes			Left for Poperinghe at 7.0 am and arrived at No 17th General Hospital at 2.0 pm	
Poperinghe	31-1-16		Workshop staff repairing Ambulances to	

H.S. Gowell. Lieut A.S.C.
O/c 24th Div F. Am. W.

24th Div
F.A.C.V.
Vol 6

Feb 1916

Army Form C. 2118.

WAR DIARY
or
INTELLIGENCE SUMMARY.
(Erase heading not required.)

Place	Date	Hour	Summary of Events and Information	Remarks and references to Appendices
No 17 Bus Clearing Station	Feb 2nd Chning to Feb 29/16.		Workshop staff carrying out repairs to Motor Ambulances, Motor Cars. Motor Cycles to as required.	

A.S. Gamwell 2nd Lieut ASC
O.C. 17th D... 7 Aux M/Shop Unit

24 Div
FAWU
Vol 7

March 1916

COMMITTEE FOR THE
MEDICAL HISTORY OF THE WAR
Date 9 - JUN 1945

Army Form C. 2118.

WAR DIARY
or
INTELLIGENCE SUMMARY.
(Erase heading not required.)

Instructions regarding War Diaries and Intelligence Summaries are contained in F. S. Regs. Part II. and the Staff Manual respectively. Title pages will be prepared in manuscript.

Place	Date	Hour	Summary of Events and Information	Remarks and references to Appendices
17. Coo Glening Str	Mch 4/16		Workshop repair Ambulances to as necessary	
- do	23.3/16	2.25	Left 17th Cas Clearing Stn carried Fletre 6.0pm	
Fletre	30.3/16	2.0pm	Left Fletre and arrived Baillieul S.13. E 76. Sheet 28.	
Baillieul	31.3/16		Workshop staff repairing Ambulances to as necessary.	

H.J. Garrett
2nd Lieut. A.S.C.
½ 24th Div. F.A.W.V